I0827469

ESSENCE

OF

NATURE

Kaiven Fenton

ISBN: 979-8-218-34985-1

Independently published

Acknowledgment

Much gratitude to my Facebook friend, Peter Baker. After reading his "Playing with Worlds" non-dual poems which I loved, I shared my poetry with him and he encouraged me to publish my poems.

CONTENTS

Winter Scenes

This day, made bright by winter's distant sun,
can be at times, so very, very cold.
This oak tree, once alive with budding limbs,
is now so desolate, bleak, and barren.
These fleecy clouds, so many miles away
turn loose their flaky holdings around us.
These meadows, now blanketed by winter,
were once alive with animals of summer.
This chilly wind, preceding icy calm,
sails laden clouds on to blot out winter's sun,
and send a spotless covering down on earth's
gloomy fields.

~ winter 1956 age 17 ~
(A high school poem assignment)

***

The following poems mirror and express my most
significant inner change and growth,
beginning in my forties.

The Tree that was

The great Palm tree
that stood so
straight and tall,
no more exists!
They cut it down
and broke it up
and hauled it all away

As if that wasn't quite
enough they came back
another day to hack
away at it's strong roots
whose job it was to
to nourish and support

No matter now,

the tree is gone

no need for any roots.

Hack away and hack some more

It's not so easy getting roots,

not as easy as the tree

Roots say, "I'm
connected to this ground
I've intertwined a lot
going deeper than
you'll ever know
so you won't be able
to get all of me,
only that which you can see"

~ 1981 ~

A Cucumber Plant

Today I planted a cucumber seed,
first time for me you see
This earth is clay and not so soft
I dug and moistened it
There was some space now
for it to grow

Another day I looked around,
spotted something breaking
through the ground
Looking closer I could see the
first of two soft wrinkled leaves
cracking through this hardened soil

Pushing up and up,
because they knew they must.
I know how hard it must have been
to crack this solid earth
in a strong desire to grow,
and then expose itself
to an unknown place
in an unknown world
at a very slow pace

I marveled and I stared,
related well I did,
Eyes teared up
‘cause something knew
I wasn't different
from these leaves
As I pierced through
my hardened shell
because I knew I must, to grow
and then expose myself
to an unknown place
in my internal world
at a very slow pace

~ 1982 ~

Just Be

Slow down and look at the butterflies
Slow down and watch the bees
Life wasn't meant to scurry around
And not even look at the trees

Take time to BE and not just exist
This is what God says to me
I cannot hear unless I slow down
or it all gets lost in the wind

Where am I going and where have I been?
I can chitter and chatter all day
But what of this moment in time that we share?
Can we take time just to Be, you and me?

~ 1990 ~

This Everlasting Mystery

Wanting so much
to share what has
really happened today
Here in the garden
of my delight
in the earliest of daylight

A flower blooms
beneath my feet
giving me a special treat.
To look in awe and
wonderment of what
I almost didn't see
As I walked
beneath a tree.

If I always fail to look around

when I'm up and off the ground

I'll never ever see

that everlasting mystery

that's always present

don't you see...?

and I can capture

it for free!

~ 1995 ~

And Now I Sing

I've turned my page and now I'm here
Trying hard to conquer fear
I want to scream, I want to play
but where's my voice, it's gone away
Go find myself so I can shout
and tell the world what I'm about

Come now I say, get up today
No, no I can't, I'm too afraid,
Patiently wait for God to come
and show me a way
to get myself up off the ground
and stop just running round and round

Rise up and fly and hear and see
Step out and feel the ocean breeze
and point your eyes up toward the sky
just go and do it...don't ask why
Express yourself out to the world
let all the might in you unfurl

I crept and crawled and now I stand
Looking out across this land
My legs are weak, but I am strong
It feels so right, it can't be wrong
I rise and jump and try my wings
I've found my voice and now I sing

~ 1999 ~

Awakening

(a 10 minute poem assignment)

Not long ago I was walking through fire
With flames all around me getting higher and higher
My whole body just burned with desire
to rise in the air going higher and higher
Where the wind and the rain would put out the flames
And I could float back to earth feeling peace not afire

My dream has come true, I feel not the flames
But a sense of contentment which was always my aim
I can walk, I can run and have fun in the sun
Go here and go there and go anywhere
I can live in my skin without any despair
Now that I'm free of the flames in my hair
I can climb up high mountains or I can swim low
Now I have confidence wherever I go

~ September 2002 ~

Silent Message

She's awfully pretty
Sitting across from me on the veranda
A warm comfortable evening
Sipping beverages
Her shimmering blue eyes shining at me
Her smile genuine, alive

I ramble on using all the words I can think of
About work, travel, school
Her verbal responses, minimal at best.
Now her gaze is steady
Face glowing in a prolonged moment

I marvel at the beauty of her eyes
as she waits for my response
Looking up, I pretend a thought
hoping she won't notice
I'm frightened by her question

She speaks a forgotten language
I’ve not spoken for eons
Rusty though I am,
I blurt out my response
“You're awfully pretty”

But she cannot hear me
The evening is over
I’m by myself
I waited too long to reply

~ September 2005 ~

Sara's Song

The girl I play "castle"
and dolls with
likes the funny faces I make
When she dresses up
like a princess
and puts on a crown
I'm moved more
then words can express

I love every part
of your dear little heart
From your head to your toes
and back up to your nose
You certainly are
my special little girl

And when we're apart
you'll always be treasured
and near and dear to my heart.

Grammy ~ 2007

I Have What I Want

My life yesterday was unconscious
The things I had were not enough
I had not attained what others had
I wanted more for myself

My life today is a conscious one
The things I have are enough
I want what I have
and I have what I want

~ 2008 ~

Dying Ego

Ladder slips
crash landing
emergency room
broken back and shoulder

Old life ends
new life begins
acceptance, fear
grief, mourning

Trusting a different path
awaiting beginnings
greeting the dawn
of the unknown

Feeling the power
of the Universe birthing me,
sisters and brothers
animals, fish and birds

Together united
connected are we
guided by a magnificent
mighty power

Ego is dying
no longer in charge
Spirit is flowing
where ego once was

~ May 2009 ~

This Moment

Not needing to please

No need to impress

Simply to be

Just to be me

My friend is the Spirit

I am the Beloved

I long to be with IT

IT comes from above

Always remember

come back to this place

which is present right here

and puts a smile on my face

This moment is all
that ever really exists
A comfortable wonderful
space of delight

Mind empties out,
All thoughts take a bow
Leaving me a pure
joy of existence
in the presence of Now

~ 2009 ~

Enough

Withholding judgments

Not speaking thoughts

Not trying to impress

Not needing to share my story

Feeling safe in my being

Knowing within

I am loving and kind

I am happy

This is enough

~ 2010 ~

Sitting in Joy

Sunny moments
at the kitchen table
mindfully eating omelet
Being present
feeling content
thankful
Spirit singing
Peace

~2010 ~

Springtime Snow

Rhodies in bloom
at Hendrick's Park
beauty surrounding
fog rolling in
under a darkening sky
splash on the windshield

Tiny hail dancing in the street
among blooming cherry trees
with snowflakes falling
blown by the wind
on flowers and trees
whether blooming or not
in a brief midwinter snowstorm
on a Spring day in March

~ 2010 ~

Life's Lessons

I can't be funny, but
I learned how to maintain good health.
I love to dance and I love to sing
I'm happy being able to see
each person's Essence
behind barriers they may put up
caring how others feel
and what their needs are
listening without judgement
when someone speaks
giving from my heart
without any measure
loving from my Soul
and arriving at joy
with contentment, peace
and tranquility

Most important lessons include
ceasing judging and criticizing
detaching from everything
switching problems to challenges
living in the present moments
giving up hopes, dreams,
anticipations and expectations

Biggest gifts come from
people I don't like much and
accepting what is here Now
Personal suffering ends.
These are the gifts I received
thus far in this wonderful
School of Life

~ Dec. 2010 ~

Moving Day...."The Shift"

(a metaphorical house / an internal shift)

The rooms in my solid house
had a wonderful egoistical flavor
The letters EGO hung over my front door
Just inside was my angry, fighting room
where lots of destruction and injury took place
Across from it was the judgmental, negative attitude room
which was somewhat smaller, but not by much
Off to the side in the back was the distant, isolation room
Where most of my time was spent hiding
Upstairs were the perfection, control and fix-it rooms
I liked it up there; I felt lots of power.
The attic was the most cluttered
I called it my selfish room
Up there was a bunch of emotional unavailability,
rigidity, pretense and intensity of an unconscious nature
Then down in the basement where I rarely went
two dusty old boxes were stored on the shelf
I'd kept them with me ever since I was young
In fact so long I'd forgotten about them

This day I looked at them more closely
One labeled Vulnerability, the other labeled Trust
Hesitantly peering inside
I recognized my precious lost friends.
Embracing them both right here on this spot
they flooded my Being and grabbed at my thoughts
The way I'd been living began to crumble
I immediately felt my house swaying then rumbling
I held on to my boxes and ran out just in time
to see my once rugged strong house
fall flat to the ground

***

“Excuse me Ma’am, I need your help
My world's crumbling around me
I’m downright scared...no terrified,
You see my once strong sturdy house
has suddenly crumbled; fell flat to the ground.
It was built for a lifetime, lived in it for ages.”
Please let me come in I’ve nowhere to go
Your house is not as big or as strong,
but it’s still standing and mine is all gone

Why, your windows are crooked
and your floors are so old,
yet I feel warmth freely flowing,
which feels so inviting.
I'd never felt warmth in my house like this
You love it here don't you, I can sense that you do
"Yes", she said with a smile on her lips
"Come I will show you around if you wish."
Here in this room I call sweet disposition.
people gather, hug and share recognition
Over there is my nurturance and intimacy room
In it we share empathy, forgiveness
and often do soul work
Then this room here is called acceptance
where we feel belonging,
closeness and lots of affection
Out there is the room I like to call play
where we do fun things, with humor and spontaneity
Far out in that corner, the creativity room
In there is self-expression, challenge and discovery
Upstairs we have the security room
where support, understanding and compassion abounds

And over here is the autonomy room
where we make choices and speak out our mind
"Let us go to the attic, nothing's up there right now,
so you can put down your boxes if you'd like,
It's your room now, open them whenever you want"
"No, no I'm afraid. When I opened them last time
my whole house collapsed!"
She said, "You're welcome to stay as long as you wish
I think you will find this house quite a treat."
After she finished showing me 'round
I looked at my new room and settled right down

Nothing happened as I opened my boxes
I put them near me on a small shelf
How did I get to such a wonderfully safe place?
I asked this of my once terrified self
then knew immediately this was my real home

When I remembered my house that collapsed
I realized I had fear like a scared little cat
But then I trusted, knocked on a strange door,
became vulnerable as never before
Begging for help I was surprised and let in

Lucky am I to have found so much courage
or I'd never have made it to this beautiful home
I'd still be afraid of this and of that
But grateful am I to have lost my old house,
because now I feel safe
to further explore
what's here in *this* place
which has become my new Home

~ 2011 ~

Amazing Lilacs

I saw your beauty,
loved your fragrance,
wanted you to grace my home.
Your many blooms gave me pleasure
with beautiful color and tiny petals
providing me a pleasant sight

I ripped you from your graceful place,
no thought of you my sweetest blooms
your death did not compute with me
until I got you home

Now I must apologize
for ending your sacred life
the one you had on your parent bush
taking in the sun and rain,
swaying softly in the breeze
waving and nodding to all your friends

Now you only have two sisters
with whom you'll slowly die
with only water to nourish you
in your last few days

I apologize for my carelessness
I feel the pain of what I've done
in an unconscious act
within a brief moment when
I saw your beauty and took it
for my own selfish pleasure,
I'm truly very sorry

~ 2011 ~

Now

In a backyard
with trees…lots of trees
and chirping birds,
a dog barks between
guitar playing and singing

Through a gentle breeze
sun warms an upturned face
as leaves create shadows
on closed eyelids
A very distant train whistle
signals the presence of NOW

~ 2011 ~

Life's Cycle

Autumn brings new delights
for my senses to take in,
thoroughly connected,
blending into the
cycle of life and death.

Fresh crisp air,
gentle breezes,
trees surrounding me
as their "children" leaves
come loose from "mother" tree
that gave them life last spring.

Buds they once were,
unfolding into new life,
gradually growing
from light to deep green,
taking in the sunlight,
giving us oxygen to breathe

Fading now in Fall,
dying to what they once were,
sailing earthbound
like a gentle rain
in full crimson colors
of red, gold and orange,
to their final resting place
for return to Mother earth

I listen to the rustle,
my life turning crimson,
fading into my Fall
My beauty shines
as my love and deeds
pour forth for others
less fortunate,
while I await my final
fall and return
to Mother earth

~ 2012 ~

Love

Empty of food,
my belly sends signals
empty of thoughts,
peace enters the space
welcoming the Now

Twilight slowly descends
while birds call out
their last good night trills
and the gentle breath of God
flows over my prone body

In grateful silence,
serene within
an unguarded moment
brings a brief flood of tears
erupting with the recognition
of God's presence
infusing my heart with Love

~ 2012 ~

Stillpoint Within

This festival day of
living many levels in chorus
healing more than ever thought
joy, gladness, pain and sorrow
coming in the space of a few moments

Languages of Native peoples,
Grandmothers and ancient wisdom,
prayers and drums of forgotten cultures
drawing deep memories and emotions
to the surface

Being with everyone
living this moment now
and that moment next
a blue heron, a flute, a flute player
entering my soul unexpectedly
knowing we are all One
loving together

Wind and sky, clouds and birds
participating fully in my being
while a luminous half moon hangs
suspended midway over
detailed designs of
Douglas fir treetops
against a sapphire blue sky

My mind is lost
in the stillpoint of my soul
where quiet emotions pull
the beauty inside out
wetting my eyes with love

~ 2012 ~

Mountains Speak

What can you tell me mountains?
You soothe me, you heal me
What else can you tell me
that I don't already know
since you've been here for
millions of years and
I'm here for a tiny spell

Mountains dwarf me
trees surround me
animals are a part of me
rivers flow through me
I am vegetation and we
are all called Life
expressing out the beauty
of our internal Love

I sit silently by
hearing the whispers of
all the secrets of the universe
and how we came to be

~ 2012 ~

Identity

I am female,

yet male flows through me

I am strong, yet I am weak

I am courageous, yet I am afraid

I love females, yet I love males

I am patient

I am steadfast

I AM Spirit

~ 2012 ~

A Summer Rain

Out on my trailer porch,
the smell of forest rain
gently sifts through my nostrils
while I quietly sit in one
of my cozy chairs becoming lost
in the trees in front of me

The sound of summer rain
lightly patters on my awning.
This water knows nothing of
its great significance to life.

Feelings of awe and
respect wash over me.
Water, trees and I are One.

Overcome with joy
at the mystery of it all,
from this Being suddenly erupts
warm water,
flooding my eyes with Love

~ August 2013 ~

Kimmy

This blanket I have sewn for you
is woven out of love
the colors of a rainbow
bending over from above

I also added something else
along with special care
a piece of gold so hidden
you may not even know is there

A mother's love is oh so strong
once allowed to sing
It's swirling all around you Kim
even when you sleep

It's in everything you ever drink,
and every book you read
When you're near the ocean
my love is in the breeze

When you feel it raining
it's my kisses on your face
claiming your attention
for a very sweet embrace

My love is in the sunlight
as you lie upon the sand
giving you the comfort
of a mother's loving hand

You came to me my Kimberly
from a million swimming sperms
You won that great big final race
with all its twists and turns

So give yourself a great big hug
and believe it came from me
wrapped in special packaging
and sent to you for free

I thank you oh so very much
for being in my world
My arms and hands enfold you
as if you were a child

You're always in a special place
just resting in my heart
I love you like a kitten
I found lost out in the dark

~ 2013 ~

Winter Walk

These woods of mine delight me so
especially in the winter snow
The peace and quiet make me feel
that what's within me is quite real

As I walk along my favorite trails
seeing tracks of deer toenails
makes me know beyond a doubt
that others here take my same route

~ 2014 ~

My Truth

I have so much more than some folks
yet not as much as others
What does it matter in the long run
when everything is done?

I know the Truth of what I AM
and emptiness abounds
What I have is peace of mind
and clouds of joy around

Material things matter least
when compared to what's inside,
for in there rests a peaceful Love
where only God resides

~ 2014 ~

The Rainstorm

A torrential downpour
pulls me out to my porch
It gathers speed and noise
Louder and louder, splashing
water on my trailer awning
Life giving water
quenching the thirst
of the great trees

Suddenly I am looking
up and into the
tall Douglas firs
that are my backyard
Their mighty trunks
together standing
with all their
outstretched branches

Torrents of water
on the way to the ground
form an engaging grey mist
hanging in and among
dark trunks and limbs

Overwhelmed by the beauty,
tears gushing from unknown
sources wetting my face,
so many tears, but I'm not sad

I look above me
The noise is deafening
The awning is stopping
the water from drenching me
I am my awning
I am protecting me
and I feel loved

More water from inside
flowing over my cheeks
Mind wants to know why,
Spirit can't explain
There are only tears
and feelings of Love

Looking back into the
steady haze of the trees
my gaze is held as a
feeling of Oneness enfolds me

I am the chair opposite me
I am the life giving rain,
the oh, so beautiful trees
There is nothing I am not
I am everything and I am loved

~ Sept. 2014 ~

A Symphony of Raindrops

Walking in the forest
in a very light rain,
I come upon one of my
favorite spots.

Stopping for a while,
basking in the moment,
something about being here
intrigues me, something
about the rain maybe

But I'm almost home
so I continue on.
Then Spirit calls me back
to sit and discover just
what was so captivating.
I return with my favorite
chair to sit with my feet up

Listening quietly,
I soon discover I am in the
middle of a symphony;
a symphony of raindrops
landing on many
flat leaved low bushes
in front of me, behind and
on each side of me,
creating a stereo effect.

Hundreds of droplets
landing with their own
unique sounds;
creating magnificence among
intermittent calls of a bird, a water frog
and the faint drone of a distant airplane.
Blessed am I...

~ 2016 ~

Connection Tears

Sinking thoroughly
into a vast and
unnamable consciousness
of everything powerfully
flowing within this body

A sudden blissful
eruption of ecstasy,
triggers a flood
of tears along with
a soft chuckle of wonderment

~ 2016 ~

A Prayer to Nature

Oh, how I love thee
I'm engrossed in Your beauty
Embraced by Your love
Your voice is my voice
as Your silence engulfs me
ever so gently

I'm touched by Your breezes,
soothed by Your embrace
joy erupts from within,
as tears flow from without
claiming this body as Yours

~ 2017 ~

Basic Needs

I have everything now
food, water and my health is good
I have a working car,
warmth and shelter too
What more is there?
Mind is empty with nothing to fear
I have all I need...I'm content

Being grateful and thankful
for being so free
Feeling warm, fed, and sheltered
I need only just BE

~ Sept. 2017 ~

Ode to a Tree

Oh Great Tree
who's just like me. Hear
me how I love thee. Why am
I so much like you, feeling just like
you were me? The strength I see is in your
trunk, so hard and very strong, standing in a quiet
stillness. Leaves and branches sing their song to those
who hear, sharing beauty for those who see while giving
great shelter for birds and bees. So there you wait ... both
day and night, through every storm that comes along. All
comes from deep within where only roots exist
You gather nourishment
and send it up to every
single branch and leaf
My roots are strong
and I'm standing tall
nourished from deep
within, sharing beauty
and my song for those
who see and those who
hear. I offer comfort during
storms. I am also waiting here

~ 2017 ~

Eternal Silence

Have you listened to snowflakes
fall on a quiet wintery day
or watched silent clouds float by
beneath a quiet moon and stars?

Have you noticed in the
darkness, the stillness of the night
as the enormous earth spins
silently around a quiet sun?

'Tis silent Life that flows within
and around us we can see
a very quiet beauty
in the silence of the trees
while swiftly flowing rivers
empty into to quiet seas

You cannot hear apples grow
or peaches ripening
Nor can you hear
potatoes, beets and carrots
growing in the ground

You cannot hear a spider,
goldfish, worm or lizard
'cause they don't make a sound

Our hair and nails grow silently
as do growing bones
while most cuts and bruises
heal quietly themselves
and our eyes in silent stillness
can emit a quiet love

Life expresses all Her beauty
in a most soundless way
and when we know it's possible
we can do our part
and BE Life's quiet stillness
within our own head and heart

~ 2017 ~

An Afternoon Walk

Down the forest path
from where I call home
I pick up a large bird feather
with tan and white stripes

Out on to the wet black road,
fir tree needles
lie scattered where they fell
and creek waters sing
their symphony

Cloudy skies,
cool crisp air flowing
in and out of my lungs
Passing clucking, scratching,
happy chickens

On up the hill,
the joy of walking feet
A black caterpillar with
a rust colored middle
crossing the road
"No I think, you are taking a big risk.
Climb on to my feather please,"
turning her in the
opposite direction

Reversing my own direction,
a dog barks, birds chirp
The creek, which
sounded like a waterfall,
fades into the distance
leaving sounds of footsteps,
breathing, and a heartbeat
softly swishing in my ears

Tall Douglas firs
stand firm and steady
Leaves clinging to their
branches all swinging at once
A distant airplane drones
as light rain drops fall
on leaves, dancing
to their own tune

Oh, a baby deer crossing
back to Mom and sibling
My loving look at first,
changes to a sideways
glance as I pass close by
Motionless bodies,
gaze in silent stillness
at a human walking

Turning up my driveway
gravel crackling under feet,
Up and up the hill I walk
A car stops and a smiling
driver asks if I'd like a ride
Not a chance would I
pass up this walk with
Nature as my guide

~ Fall 2017 ~

Breath of God

An ease in living
how can this be?
Feeling so grateful
being so free
I flow like a river,
float like a cloud
I am merely a feather
on the breath of God

~ 2018 ~

God Singing

God sings to me
in the daylight and
from every single tree
She sings to me
a song of love
reminding me I'm free

God sings to me
from the flowers
inspiring great delight
She sings to me
from the hillside
and in the dead of night

God sings to me
from the ocean
and from the
moon and stars
She sings in
every rainstorm
She's never very far

God sings to me
when I’m weary
sounding loud and clear
She sings when
I’m not listening
knowing I am here

~ 2018 ~

Life's Song

The morning breeze is cool
air alive with Life
wind is being wind
as it tinkles little bell
Birds know what to do
They fly and sing and chirp
while all kinds of flowers wave
in silent beauty

Animals know how to be
The cat is doing cat things
Dogs are being dogs
sniffing things mostly
The chickens know to
cluck and chuckle
a chorus they can be, but
like the velvet rabbit caged
aren't out and being free

The bees know to buzz
The trees know how to be
I know human things
Like sitting drinking tea
recording the secret mystery
of the Life I hear and see

~ July 2018 ~

To a Friend

Drunk with the wine of Spirit
I fall asleep taking you with me
into the other dream.
Enjoying our other stories
in light hearted joy and delight

~ 2018 ~

Voluntary Death

Feeling as if I am on
a mountain precipice
while Nature echos all around
Shall I follow an urge and make the jump
and die on my way to the ground?

Or shall I stay safely stuffed in my skin
suffering the battles of self?
Spirit calls…step off the cliff…
the unknown is the best choice
fall into most certain death

Only what's *not* me will die, I'm told
But what does that mean I ask
Something about trust I hear in reply
Just have faith IT won't die

Risking all fear and taking the leap
right into a chasm unknown
now something is different, extremely odd
‘cause into a void I have flown

What is there here? Nothing it seems
No more of a self that was me,
only a timeless Essence remains
I've fallen Home and I’m free!

~ 2018 ~

This Life

A field of trust and natural joy
in the heart space of this Being
Body moves, mouth speaks,
actions taken, senses sense
within a field of harmony,
oneness and beauty

Peace, love, compassion,
quiet emptiness, not moving
timeless serene ineffable, this Life

~ 2018 ~

What am I?

I am that beautiful
mysteriously divine,
eternally infinite,
timeless, essence
called Life,
dwelling within and
without this body,
beating a heart,
breathing lungs,
digesting food
and animating the
limbs of that in
which I exist, as
unconditional
Love and Life

~ 2020~

Ineffable Life

Help me to express You
There's nothing here to see
Who are You really and
why do You love me

You are me and I AM You
in this here world of ours
You love me as I AM
I love You as you are

You express through blades of grass,
the rose and squirrel too
I am You the spider
We are One we are

Tears of joy are flowing
Together we are clouds
There is no here, there is no there
We're always One right here

Connected by the Essence
of the Love we truly are
sharing Life eternal
whether here or near or far

Life is one big mystery
we cannot see or touch
But we are That and only That
Can’t be any less than That

We are Life in all Her glory
expressing through our forms
not beginning, never ending
no one here knows why

You cannot find us in a book
We're only seen
by those who look
and know that they are we

Being One together with
birds and trees and bees
flowers, leaves, and butterflies
closer than intimacy

~ 2020 ~

Just Being

Like shifting sands
of Awareness….
shifting here, shifting there,
shifting into everywhere

Morning silence,
empty, calm, no mind,
peaceful, withdrawn
God is everywhere
as inner acceptance
and gratefulness

Walking,
raking up fir cones
in the forest,
sitting with friends,
a walk home,
quiet, eating

A silence falls from
everywhere, another
shift…just Being

~ 2020 ~

Morning breeze

This morning's breeze
floating on and around my bare skin,
vibrant Life surrounding me as Beauty
and felt within as Love

We're in this forest together,
absorbing You from everywhere
sharing this thing called Life

My body walks in, through and with You
knowing You intimately on every level
as I Be with You this morning

~ 2021 ~

Where am I?

I am *here*,
descended into
a quiet emptiness,
the core of Being,
an innermost niche,
intimate and indefinable,
a kind of merging with
a primal awareness
that I AM
an intangible Essence,
of unconditional Love,
within a physical body,
animating and being seen
with external eyes,
but not actually physical
I am Home...

~ 2021 ~

Why am I Here?

I am here
to free my self
from the illusion
of being separate
from the Universe
and others,
by experientially
realizing
I AM One
with all Life forms
in a cosmic
energy of Love,
not actually a part
of the physical world,
even though I must
exist in it for a time

~ 2022 ~

The Journey

My life has become
nothing less than
a beautiful inward
adventure, because
Grace led me
to look into the depths
of my Soul

I explored new places
I'd never been
or even knew existed.
Nothing left unturned,
I discovered internal
coffee shops,
many hidden streets,
climbed rugged mountains
and walked along
quiet beaches

I met people unlike me,
learned to love them all
Being in awe of Life itself
I became
"transformed by the
renewing of my mind"

~ 2022 ~

What Sees?

That which is looking
is the same
in all of humans

Internal eyes
can see and know
what is here NOW

Now is the
moment that
never ends

~ 2022 ~

What Thinks Thoughts?

What is this "I" which
thinks up thoughts and
sees with physical eyes?

Be only That which
thinks up the thoughts
and watch them all
come and go

Keep your attention on
inner "I" only, 'cause
the mystery's not very far

Ignore the
mind, or personal self
which thinks it's controlling
that "I"

You cannot touch IT,
or hear IT, or see IT
but IT's what
You eternally are!

~ 2022 ~

Oneness

Perceiving the flying,
heart beating,
air sac energy
within the bird
to be the same as the
heart beating, lung breathing,
human energy within this body

I'm overcome with the joy
of watching flying feathers
dipping here and there,
eyes flood with love,
at this miraculous
experience of Oneness

~ 2022 ~

The Mystery

Love is what YOU eternally are
even when you don't like yourself
Why you ask,
might this be so?

You are made in the image
of a Holy ineffable Spirit
Impossible to be other than That
even in a form

Mind thinks that what you are
is limbs, a spine and feet.
But you need not believe
everything you think

Mind and Spirit can't be known
in the same allotted space
So make a distance from mind now
and let thoughts go to sleep
When Spirit comes to take their place,
the benefits you'll reap

The greatest mystery of all
can now reveal ITSelf to you
Because mind no longer stands between
That mystery and YOU

~ 2022 ~

Poems

Living in and from an empty space
where deepest waters flow
no words abide in here
just wordless peace is known

How can poems spring from
such an empty place
producing from the stillness
abundant words for us to taste?

They fall from out of nowhere
arranged upon on a page
expressing out from deep within
what *they* want to say

~ 2022 ~

self or Self

Smaller self is physical
touchable, tangible,
conceptual, and visible

Larger Self is non-physical,
untouchable, non-tangible,
non-conceptual and invisible

Where is this larger Self? you ask
It is nowhere and everywhere
carried within, expressed without
as Life's Essence or Presence

IT is the You as a young child,
same as the adult You
Stop and notice that natural You
always here in the present
moments of Now

~ 2022 ~

Starlight

The breath of life
flows through my nostrils
while a breeze
gently kisses this body
sitting outside on my porch
What is this peace about?

Below are sounds of whippoorwills
above a starlit sky
To recognize this touch of God
demands that time stand still

A suffering and complaining self
can't ever truly know
how beautiful they are inside
while struggling in this life
with all it's aching throes

Only flying up and out
and hanging to a star
can they look back
and see their Self
is the truest light they are
which is not so very different
from the light of brightest stars

~ 2023 ~

Window of the Soul

When I meet you here
in the timelessness of Presence
and look into your eyes
Words are never needed

Love becomes our Essence.
But what is it that I see?
It's just your very Soul
which is looking back at me

~ 2023 ~

Essence

Surrender the identity
of who you think you are
You are nothing
and You have nothing.

If you think you do
give it all up
and BE what's left...
an exquisite, radiant
Life and Love
that can only be
your Essence

~ 2023 ~

Life

Life takes care of Life
it's energy will flow,
but only when I listen
will *it* tell me where to go

Surrendering all ideas and thoughts
and what's going on in mind
and listening to a greater source
a treasure I will find

It always comes from deep within
and knows what needs attention
Listen up and let *it* flow
Because *it's* not insentient

~ 2023 ~

What knows?

Self knows.

What self?

The inner God Self.

Is there another self?

There are two selves.

The internal God Self speaks in silence

the physical self speaks in words

How can that be?

Our brain is divided

One part expresses

as the reasoning mind self

the other part expresses

as the intuitive God Self

How so?

The physical mind self is logical
The God Self is Love without words

So what knows?

The One who knows doesn't speak
Listen to the Silence

~ 2023 ~

To a Great Love

Bliss so powerful
is nothing short of ecstasy
as I feel Your arms around me
and rest in Your embrace

The warmth of Your sunshine
brings a deep and silence space
where tears ooze from somewhere
and flow upon my face

I hear You, I feel You
inside an inner core
taking me with You
whichever way You go

I so enjoy Your welcome,
oh great and mighty Peace,
for the silence of Your closeness,
and Your warm and gentle breeze

Our Love it is eternal
and cannot ever die
Thank you, thank you, thank you
for Your soft and warm embrace
as I BE with You forever
in this eternal place

~ 2023 ~

Presence

It's not about having
the perfect psychology
or the perfect conditions.
Those are always stories or ideas,
illusions of the mind
They aren't your Truth

Rather than disappearing
in mind's illusions and
accompanying feelings,
none of which are true,
come back to what IS

Your Truth is the Peace,
and Love of what You are
deep within
This Oneness of Truth,
is here right now
beaming from the heart
in every experience...
of all there is

IT is prior to birth,
IT is here in deep sleep
and here after body death
IT is what the energy of Life is made of
IT is the formless intelligent Essence
of the physical you

beating your heart
breathing your lungs
directing all bodily processes
and sensorial perceptions

Anything else you believe is needed,
anything you think you can't live without
or you can't have, is illusionary

The only thing that's true
is the deepest
Essence of You...your heart
the Being-ness and Truth of Life,
which is here, here, here, *now*
freely with no effort,
singing in all that IS

IT is singing in this moment,
IT is singing in no place
and singing in every place

Here, outside of time,
present in the silence
present in this moment...
the one that never ends

Stay here and listen deeply...
IT will recognize your presence

~ 2023

Where is Love

A quiet glance, an unfocused gaze
through a darkened window pane
brought hidden memories of a loving past
my photos reflected in the glass

What I then began to feel
was a Love inside, I know was real
It called out from deep within
and I wanted more of IT

I *want* You God, my sudden cry
Where *are* you now, please tell me why...
"I'm in *everyone*" was the quick reply

"I can be found in every person
walking around on human feet
or just sitting on a city street
waiting for your meet and greet."

Transcendent is the Love you'll meet
beyond the physical and emotional you
that formless Love Essence deep within,
is simply recognized in another

www.ingramcontent.com/pod-product-compliance
Lightning Source LLC
LaVergne TN
LVHW090615110826
845146LV00001B/398

* 9 7 9 8 2 1 8 3 4 9 8 5 1 *